Financial Accounting (FA)

Diploma in accounting

Pocket Notes

KAPLAN
PUBLISHING

British library cataloguing-in-publication data

A catalogue record for this book is available from the British Library.

Published by:
Kaplan Publishing UK
Unit 2 The Business Centre
Molly Millars Lane
Wokingham
Berkshire
RG41 2QZ

ISBN 978-1-83996-409-1

© Kaplan Financial Limited, 2023

Printed and bound in Great Britain.

Acknowledgements

This product contains copyright material and trademarks of the IFRS Foundation®. All rights reserved. Used under licence from the IFRS Foundation®. Reproduction and use rights are strictly limited. For more information about the IFRS Foundation and rights to use its material please visit www.ifrs.org.

Disclaimer: To the extent permitted by applicable law the Board and the IFRS Foundation expressly disclaims all liability howsoever arising from this publication or any translation thereof whether in contract, tort or otherwise (including, but not limited to, liability for any negligent act or omission) to any person in respect of any claims or losses of any nature including direct, indirect, incidental or consequential loss, punitive damages, penalties or costs.

Information contained in this publication does not constitute advice and should not be substituted for the services of an appropriately qualified professional. No part of this publication may be reproduced, stored in a retrieval system, or transmitted in any form or by any means, electronic, mechanical, photocopying, recording, or otherwise, without prior written permission of Kaplan Publishing and the IFRS Foundation.

&IFRS

The IFRS Foundation logo, the IASB logo, the IFRS for SMEs logo, the 'Hexagon Device', 'IFRS Foundation', 'eIFRS', 'IAS', 'IASB', 'IFRS for SMEs', 'IASs', 'IFRS', 'IFRSs', 'International Accounting Standards' and 'International Financial Reporting Standards', 'IFRIC', NIIF® and 'SIC' are **Trade Marks** of the IFRS Foundation.

 **IFRS**

Trade Marks

The Foundation has trade marks registered around the world ('**Trade Marks**') including 'IAS®', 'IASB®', 'IFRIC®', 'IFRS®', the IFRS® logo, 'IFRS for SMEs®', IFRS for SMEs® logo, the 'Hexagon Device', 'International Financial Reporting Standards®', NIIF® and 'SIC®'.

Further details of the Foundation's Trade Marks are available from the Licensor on request.

Contents

This document references IFRS® Standards and IAS® Standards, which are authored by the International Accounting Standards Board (the Board), and published in the 2022 IFRS Standards Red Book.

Introduction

Background

The aim of ACCA Financial Accounting, is to develop knowledge and understanding of the underlying principles and concepts relating to financial accounting and technical proficiency in the use of double-entry accounting techniques including the preparation of basic financial statements.

Objective of the syllabus

- Explain the context and purpose of financial reporting.
- Define the qualitative characteristics of financial information and the fundamental bases of accounting.
- Demonstrate the use of double entry and accounting systems.
- Record transactions and events.
- Prepare a trial balance (including identifying and correcting errors).
- Prepare basic financial statements for incorporated and unincorporated entities.
- Prepare simple consolidated financial statements.
- Interpretation of financial statements.

Core areas of the syllabus

- The context and purpose of financial reporting.
- The qualitative characteristics of financial information.
- The use of double entry and accounting.
- Recording transactions and events.
- Preparing a trial balance.
- Preparing basic financial statements.
- Preparing simple consolidated statements.

Examination Format

The examination is a two-hour computer-based examination.

The assessment will contain 100% compulsory questions and will comprise the following:

Section A: 35 × 2-mark objective test questions

Section B: 2 × 15-mark multi-task questions

The Section B questions will test consolidations and accounts preparation.

Computer-based examination (CBE) – tips

Be sure you understand how to use the software before you start the exam. If in doubt, ask the assessment centre staff to explain it to you.

Questions are **displayed on the screen** and answers are entered using keyboard and mouse. At the end of the exam, you are given a certificate showing the result you have achieved.

The CBE exam will not only examine multiple choice questions but could include questions that require a single number entry or a multiple response.

Do not attempt a CBE until you have **completed all study material** relating to it. **Do not skip any of the material** in the syllabus.

To help you to prepare for your CBE examination, you should access and attempt the specimen CBE examination available on the ACCA website.

Read each question very carefully.

Double-check your answer before committing yourself to it.

Answer every question – If you do not know the answer, you don't lose anything by guessing. Think carefully before you **guess**.

The CBE question types are as follows:

*   Multiple choice – where you are required to choose one answer from a list of options provided by clicking on the appropriate 'radio button'

*   Multiple response – where you are required to select more than one response from the options provided by clicking on the appropriate tick leave space to show highlighted words as: boxes (typically choose two options from the available list)

- Multiple response matching – where you are required to indicate a response to a number of related statements by clicking on the 'radio button' which corresponds to the appropriate response for each statement
- Number entry – where you are required to key in a response to a question shown on the screen.

Note that the CBE variant of the examination will not require you to input text, although you may be required to choose the correct text from options available.

Don't panic if you realise you've answered a question incorrectly. Getting one question wrong will not mean the difference between passing and failing.

Quality and accuracy are of the utmost importance to us so if you spot an error in any of our products, please send an email to mykaplanreporting@kaplan.com with full details, or follow the link to the feedback form in MyKaplan.

Our Quality Co-ordinator will work with our technical team to verify the error and take action to ensure it is corrected in future editions.

Glossary

Accounting records	Any listing or book which records the transactions of a business in a logical manner.
Accrued expense	An expense which has been incurred but not paid by the end of the accounting period.
Asset expenditure	Expenditure on acquiring or improving non-current assets for use in the business and not for resale. Reported in the statement of financial position.
Credit note	Records goods returned by a customer or the reduction of monies owed by a customer.
Current asset	Assets which the business intends to use, sell, or change regularly in the normal course of business. E.g. inventory, receivables and cash.
Current liability	A liability which is payable within 12 months of the reporting date.
Debit note	Sometimes raised by a purchaser of goods. It is a formal request for a credit note to be issued by the supplier.
Duality	Every transaction has two effects. This underpins double entry and the statement of financial position.
Financial accounting	Concerned with accounting to users **outside** the enterprise for the way in which the business's funds have been used. Done by presenting a statement of financial position and statement of profit or loss, usually on an annual basis.

Financial management	Seeks to ensure that financial resources are obtained and used in the most effective way to secure attainment of the objectives of the organisation. It is largely to do with the management of cash and investments.
Expenditure	Expenditure on acquiring current assets, on running the enterprise and on maintaining non-current assets. Reported in the statement of profit or loss. It is also referred to as revenue expenditure.
Historical cost	All values are based on the historical costs incurred.
Ledger accounts	Also known as 'T' accounts. Pages in a book (the ledger) with a separate page reserved for transactions of the same type.
Management accounting	An integral part of management activity inside the enterprise, concerned with identifying, presenting and interpreting detailed information used for formulation of strategy, planning and controlling activities, decision taking and optimising the use of resources.
Materiality	If information could influence users' decisions taken on the basis of financial statements it is material.
Neutrality	If information is free of deliberate or systematic bias it is considered to be neutral.
Non-current asset	Any asset, tangible or intangible, acquired for retention by an entity for the purpose of providing a service to the business, and not held for resale in the normal course of trading.

Non-current liability	A liability which is payable more than 12 months after the reporting date.
Prepayment	An expense which has been paid in advance for a period which extends beyond the end of the current accounting period.
Prudence	The exercise of caution when making judgments under conditions of uncertainty. In particular, income and assets should not be overstated and expenses and liabilities should not be understated.
Provision	An amount written off to provide for the diminution in value of an asset (e.g. a provision for depreciation) or an amount retained to provide for a known liability whose amount cannot be determined with accuracy. A provision is treated as an expense in the statement of profit or loss.
Purchase order	An agreement to purchase goods/services from a business. It is prepared by the purchaser.
Sales invoice	A formal record of the amount of money due from the customer as a result of the sale transaction.
Sales order	An agreement to sell goods/services to a business. It is prepared by the seller.
Source document	An individual record of a business transaction.

Statement of financial position	A statement of assets, liabilities and equity at a point in time.
Statement of cash flows	Provides information about cash receipts and cash payments during an accounting period.
Statement of profit or loss and other comprehensive income.	A summary of income and expenditure for a period of time, showing the profit or loss made in an accounting period, together with any items of other comprehensive income arising in the same accounting period.
Time interval	Also known as the **accounting period convention**. The lifetime of the business is divided into arbitrary periods of a fixed length, usually one year, and referred to as the accounting period.

1

Introduction to financial reporting

In this chapter

- Users of financial statements.
- Sole trader v limited company.
- The regulatory framework.
- Elements of the financial statements.
- Qualitative characteristics of useful financial information.
- Other accounting concepts.

Users of financial statements

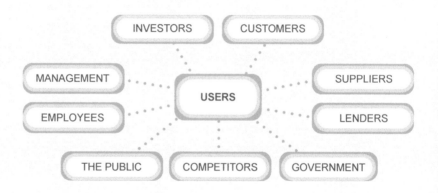

Sole trader v limited company

	Sole trader	Limited company
Legal background	Little statutory control over a sole trader's business. **No** legal requirement for the **public disclosure** of accounting information.	Required to comply with Companies Acts requirements. **Accounting information** and details of directors and shareholders must usually be made public.
Legal status	**Not a separate legal entity** from the proprietor as an individual. All the assets and rights belonging to the business and all the liabilities of the business are those of the proprietor personally.	A company constitutes a **separate legal entity** from its owners, the shareholders. A company can own assets, owe money, enter contracts, and sue or be sued in a court of law as a legal person, separate from its owners.
Owner's liability	The **proprietor has unlimited personal liability** to the payables of the business, to the full extent of his or her private as well as business assets.	The **liability of the owners** (the shareholders) is **limited** to the company's own assets plus any uncalled share capital. If the shares are fully paid and the company becomes insolvent, the shareholders have no further liability for the unpaid debts of the company.

	Sole trader (contd)	Limited company (contd)
Audit	**No annual audit** is required.	An **annual audit is usually required**.
Management	The owner **normally manages the business**, although this is not always the case.	Often, **shareholders do not run the company** themselves but **appoint directors to do so**. (Shareholders may, of course, also be directors, and many smaller companies are run by shareholder-directors).

The regulatory framework

Need for regulation	Role of IFRS Standards
• Regulation ensures that accounts are sufficiently reliable and useful, and prepared without unnecessary delay. • Financial accounts are used as the starting point for calculating taxable profits. • The annual report and accounts is the main document used for reporting to shareholders on the condition and performance of a company. • The stock markets rely on the published financial statements by companies. • International investors prefer information to be presented in a similar and comparable way, no matter where the company is based.	• IFRS Standards aim to harmonise as far as possible the different accounting standards and accounting policies of different countries, and to provide a framework for financial reporting that can be adopted by all countries. • They don't have the force of law. They are only effective if adopted by the national regulatory bodies. • Many countries have changed and adapted their national accounting standards to comply with or be consistent with IFRS Standards. • Companies whose shares are traded on the stock market are often required to issue financial statements that comply with IFRS Standards.

The **IFRS Foundation** is the supervisory body to the IASB and is responsible for governance and funding.

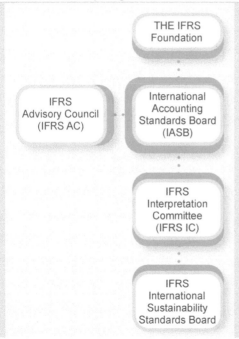

- The **International Accounting Standards Board (IASB)** is responsible for developing and issuing new International Financial Reporting Standards.

- The **IFRS IC** issues rapid guidance where there are differing interpretations of IASs/IFRSs.

- The **IFRS AC** advises the IASB in developing new standards.

- The **IFRS ISSB** was formed with the objective to produce comprehensive sustainability-related disclosure standards.

The objectives of the IFRS Foundation are to:

- develop, in the public interest, a single set of high-quality accounting standards
- promote the use and rigorous application of those standards
- bring about the convergence of national accounting standards and international accounting standards.

Procedure for the development of an IFRS	
• The IASB identifies an aspect of accounting for which a new standard or a revision to an existing standard might be required.	• The IASB sets out the concepts that underlie the preparation and presentation of financial statements for external users in the **Conceptual Framework for Financial Reporting 2018**.
• The IASB then appoints an **advisory group** to advise on the project.	• International financial reporting standards are developed within this conceptual framework.
• A **discussion document** is prepared and issued for public comment.	• The **Framework** is not an accounting standard.
• The IASB then publishes an **exposure draft** for public comment.	• Nothing in the **Framework** can override a specific IAS or IFRS.
• Following the consideration of comments, the IASB publishes final text of the IFRS.	

The objective of financial statements is to provide information about:

- the **financial position** of an enterprise (provided mainly in the **statement of financial positio**
- its **financial performance** (provided mainly in the **statement of profit or loss and other comprehensive income**), and
- changes in its financial position (provided in a separate financial statement) that is useful to a wide range of users in making 'economic decisions'.

Underlying assumption in the Framework
Going concern basis
'The financial statements of an enterprise are prepared on the assumption that it is a going concern and will continue in operation for the foreseeable future' (Framework, Para 4.1).

Elements of the financial statements

Financial position – shown in the statement of financial position	
Statement of financial position = a statement of assets, liabilities and equity at a certain point in time.	
Asset	A present economic resource controlled by the entity as a result of past events e.g. buildings, inventory, trade receivables.
Liability	A present obligation of the entity to transfer an economic resource as a result of past events e.g. bank loan or overdraft, trade payables.
Equity	The residual interest in the assets after deducting all the liabilities from the total assets. Also known as capital.
Financial performance – statement of profit or loss and other comprehensive income.	
Statement of profit or loss and other comprehensive income. = a summary of income and expenditure over a period of time.	
Income	Increases in assets, or decreases in liabilities, that result in increases in equity, other than those relating to contributions from the holders of equity claims.
Expense	Decreases in assets, or increases in liabilities, that result in decreases in equity, other than those relating to distributions to holders of equity claims.

Qualitative characteristics of useful financial information

Qualitative characteristics of financial information are the qualities that make the information useful to its users. The IASB's Framework identifies two fundamental qualitative characteristics and four enhancing qualitative characteristics.

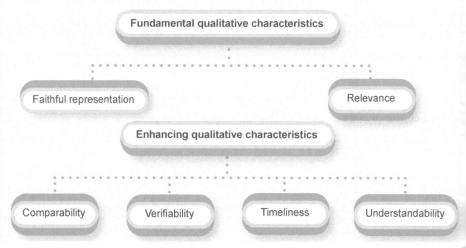

Relevance	Information is relevant if it capable of making a difference in the decisions made by users. This is likely to be the case when information can be used to confirm current understanding and/or to or predict future outcomes.
	Materiality is one aspect of relevance – information is **material** if its omission or misstatement could influence the decisions of users of the financial statements.
Faithful representation	Information should be faithfully represented. This means that accounting information should be presented in accordance with best practice and that the commercial substance of transactions should be presented in the financial statements, rather than their strict legal form. This would imply that such information is complete, neutral or free from bias and free from material error.
Comparability	Users must be able to compare the financial statements of an enterprise over time to identify trends in its financial position and performance.
	Users must also be able to compare the financial statements of **different enterprises** to evaluate their relative financial positions, performance and financial adaptability.
Verifiability	Information should be capable of either direct verification or indirect verification.
Timeliness	This means that users of information have access to that information within timescales which are appropriate for their decision-making purposes.
Understandability	Information in financial statements must be understandable to its users. This may depend upon how knowledgeable individuals are when evaluating financial information.

Other accounting concepts

Accruals	This means that transactions are recorded when revenues are earned and when expenses are incurred, which may be different to when cash is actually received or paid in relation to a transaction.
Business entity concept	Transactions are recorded as if the business is separate and distinct from its owners. Consequently, any transactions between the business and the business owners (e.g. drawings and capital introduced) are treated differently to business-related transactions (e.g. purchases and sales).
Consistency	Items in the financial statements should be classified and presented in a consistent manner throughout an accounting period, and from one accounting period to another.
Going concern	Financial statements are prepared on the presumption that the business will continue to operate and trade for the foreseeable future. If this presumption is not applicable, the financial statements should be prepared on a 'break-up' or liquidation basis.
Materiality	Items which are regarded as material should be presented or disclosed separately in the financial statements. This will help users to gain a proper understanding of the transactions, balances and events which have affected the financial statements.

Prudence	The exercise of caution when making judgments under conditions of uncertainty. Income and assets should not be overstated. Liabilities and expenses should not be understated. Prudence supports the principle of neutrality when preparing financial statements to help ensure fair presentation of information.
Substance over form	The economic substance of transactions should be reflected in the financial statements. This is important as, when there is a conflict with the legal form of a transaction, its economic substance should be reflected.
Stewardship	The management of resources by business managers on behalf of the business owners - the managers are accountable to the business owners.

You need to be able to define and apply the various concepts and terms covered in this chapter as they are frequently examined.

The ACCA FA syllabus and exam presumes that businesses use integrated computerised accounting systems. Note that the bank account is presumed NOT to be part of the integrated accounting system.

2

Bookkeeping principles

In this chapter

- The accounting equation.
- Double entry.
- Double entry checklist.
- Balancing the accounts.
- The trial balance.

This chapter lays the foundations for the whole syllabus, so it's important you get to grips with it. Double entry and financial statements will appear in every examination. The examiner has specifically stated that this is a vital topic.

The accounting equation

Assets – Liabilities = Capital

Assets = Liabilities + Capital

The accounting equation illustrates the point that each transaction has a double effect on the accounting equation. This is known as the dual aspect of transactions, and underlies double entry book-keeping. **After each transaction the accounting equation will always be equal.**

Double entry

The 'T' accounts (ledger accounts) should be set out as follows:

The details column tells you which account contains the other half of the double entry.

Debit side ↓		Cash account			Credit side
Date	Details	$	Date	Details	$
1/1/X6	Capital	1,000			

		Capital account			
Date	Details	$	Date	Details	$
			1/1/X6	Cash	1,000

Double entry checklist

This checklist details the most common business transactions.

It shows you which account must be debited and which must be credited.

Transaction	Debit	Credit
Purchase of non-current asset for cash	Non-current asset	Cash
Purchase of non-current asset on credit	Non-current asset	Trade payable
Purchase of inventory for cash	Purchases (not inventory)	Cash
Purchase of inventory on credit	Purchases	Trade payable
Return of inventory bought on credit to supplier	Trade payable	Purchase returns
Sale of inventory for cash	Cash	Sales
Sale of inventory on credit	Trade receivable	Sales
Customer returns goods bought on credit	Sales returns	Trade receivable
Payment to supplier	Trade payable	Cash
Receipt from customer	Cash	Trade receivable
Payment of expense in cash	Expense	Cash
Cash received as a loan	Cash	Loan
Rent received from sub-letting premises	Cash	Rent received

Balancing the accounts

Step 1 Add up the total debits and credits in the account and make a note of the totals.

Step 2 Insert the **higher** total at the bottom of both the debits and credits, leaving one line for the inclusion of a **balance c/d** (carried down).

The totals should be level with each other and underlined.

Step 3 Insert on the side which has the lower arithmetical total, the narrative 'balance c/d' and an amount which brings the arithmetical total to the total that has been inserted under step 2 above.

Step 4 The same figure is shown on the other side of the ledger account but **underneath** the totals. This is the **balance b/d** (brought down).

The trial balance

A Business – Trial balance as at 31 March 20X6

Account	Debit $	Credit $
Share capital		x
Cash	x	
Non-current asset	x	
Purchases	x	
Revenue		x
Trade payables		x
Trade receivables	x	
Rent	x	
Loan		x
Insurance	x	
	x	x

The trial balance should be headed with the name of the business and the date.

Only balances brought down are listed.

Assets, expenses and drawings are debit balances.

Income, liabilities and capital are credit balances.

Both sides of the trial balance should add up to the same figure. The totals should be level with each other and underlined.

3

Recording transactions

In this chapter

- Stages of accounting.
- Journals.
- Petty cash record.
- Receipts into the bank account.
- Payments from the bank account.
- Discounts.
- Variable consideration.
- Sales tax.

Ensure that you understand the flow of information from the source documents to the financial statements. Learn the items that will appear in each of the relevant book of prime entry. Ensure that you can calculate discounts and sales tax.

Stages of accounting

	Stage 1	**Stage 2**	
TRANSACTIONS	JOURNALS	LEDGER ACCOUNTS	FINANCIAL STATEMENTS

General ledger	Receivables/sales and payables/purchases ledgers
Contains all the **double entry** accounts – i.e. asset, liability, income and expense accounts. Includes accounts receivable and accounts payable accounts. These are ledger accounts which summarise a large number of transactions.	Subsidiary or **memorandum ledgers** which record detailed transactions and allow staff to identify individual supplier (payable) and customer (receivable) balances. They are separate from the general ledger and are **not usually part of the double entry**. They are basically a list of outstanding amounts due to/from the company that can be used to schedule payments and chase unpaid debts.

Journals

Journal	Transaction dealt with	General ledger		Accounts payable or receivable ledger
		Debit	Credit	
Purchases	Invoices for goods or services purchased from suppliers on credit	Expenditure accounts e.g. purchases, light and heat, telephone	Accounts payable ledger account	Entered on supplier's personal account on 'credit' side on individual basis
Sales	Invoices for goods to customers on credit	Accounts receivable ledger account	Revenue accounts e.g. sales, sundry income, rental income	Entered on customer's personal account on 'debit' side on individual basis
Purchases returns	Credit notes for goods returned to suppliers	Accounts payable ledger account	Purchases returns	Entered on supplier's personal account on 'debit' side on individual basis
Sales returns	Credit notes for goods returned by customers	Sales returns	Accounts receivable ledger account	Entered on customer's personal account on 'credit' side on individual basis

The receivables and payables accounts in the general ledger show the total of transactions and balances relating to credit sales and credit purchases.

Separate receivables' and payables' ledgers are maintained (not part of the double-entry system) that contain the record of account and transactions for each customer and supplier respectively.

Example

As an example, if this approach were adopted by a business, the entries for purchases would be as follows. The amended entries are shown in bold.

	Transaction dealt with	General ledger		Receivables or payables ledger account
		Debit	**Credit**	
Purchases	Invoices for goods or services purchased from suppliers on credit	Expenditure accounts e.g. purchases, light and heat, telephone	**Trade payables**	**Payables ledger account**

Petty cash record

- The petty cash system is designed to deal with sundry small payments in cash, e.g. purchasing biscuits, buying stationery or reimbursing travelling expenses.

- Petty cash record – **posted to** the petty cash ledger account in the **general ledger**.

- An **imprest** system works as follows

  - Establish a float of a set amount. (Dr petty cash, Cr bank).

  - Record payments from petty cash in the petty cash record. Each payment should be backed by a voucher prepared by the petty cashier.

  - Total the petty cash record and post the payments made to the relevant accounts in the general ledger. (Dr stationery/travel/sundry, Cr petty cash.)

  - Withdraw cash from the bank account to return the petty cash to the amount of the float.

- At any stage the petty cash float should be represented in the petty cash box by actual cash + any vouchers in support of payments made since the last reimbursement.

Receipts into the bank account

Date	Detail	Ledger Ref	Bank	Receivables Ledger	Cash sales	Rental income	Sundry income
			$	$	$	$	$
2 Feb	Cash sales		140		140		
5 Feb	S Black	B7	75	75			
9 Feb	J Clark		5				5
16 Feb	Cash sales		100		100		
23 Feb	B Brown	B8	16	16			
24 Feb	Hire-it Ltd		80			80	
27 Feb	J Purple	P6	5	5			
			421	96	240	80	5

The figures in the 'bank' column are the **debit** entries in the double entry system.

The totals of these four columns will be posted to the **credit** of the other ledger accounts.

Payments from the bank account

Date	Detail	Cheque No	Ledger ref	Bank	Discount received	Payables Ledger	Wages	Petty cash	Sundry expenses
				$	$	$	$	$	$
2 Feb	Wages	124507	–	1,052			1,052		
5 Feb	J Smith	124508	S13	58	1	58			
9 Feb	B Jones	124509	–	120					120
16 Feb	Cash	124510	–	150				150	
23 Feb	S Green	124511	G7	80	6	80			
24 Feb	B Orange	124512	O17	100		100			
27 Feb	D Brown	124513	B13	119	2	119			
				1,679	9	357	1,052	150	120

The figures in the 'bank' column are the **credit** entries in the double entry system.

The totals of these four columns will be posted to the **debit** of the other ledger accounts.

The discount column is a memorandum (i.e. the entry in the cash book is not part of the double entry). The double entry is recorded by Dr Payables control (and individual supplier's account) Cr Discounts received.

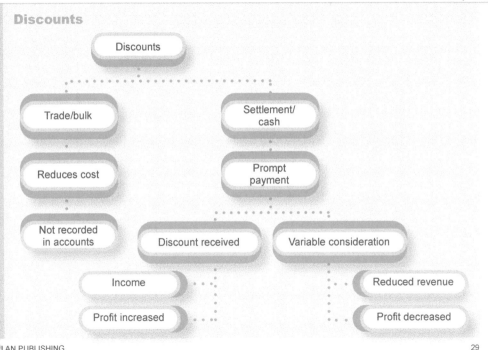

Discounts

- Discounts
  - Trade/bulk
    - Reduces cost
      - Not recorded in accounts
  - Settlement/cash
    - Prompt payment
      - Discount received
        - Income
        - Profit increased
      - Variable consideration
        - Reduced revenue
        - Profit decreased

Term	Relates to	Bookkeeping implications	Recorded initially in
Cash discount received	Discount for payment to a supplier before a stated date.	Purchases are debited with the full invoice price (e.g. $100). On payment to the supplier, the difference between the cash paid and the full invoice price represents the cash discount received. E.g. Dr Payables $100, Cr Cash $95, Cr Discount received $5.	Memorandum note with bank payment made and then recorded in the general ledger.
Trade discount	Favourable price for people in the same trade.	Sales/purchases are recorded at trade price (i.e. the lower price involved). The amount of the discount does not appear in the ledger accounts.	Invoice

Variable consideration

When goods are sold on credit, the seller must estimate the amount of revenue that will be receivable. Trade discount is always deducted in arriving at the price to be invoiced. If early settlement terms are offered to the customer, the seller must estimate whether or not it is probable that the early settlement terms offered will be taken by the customer.

If it is probable that early settlement will be made by the customer, then early settlement discount should be deducted in arriving at the invoice price.

If it is probable that early settlement will not be made by the customer, early settlement discount is not deducted in arriving at the invoice price.

When cash is subsequently received from the customer, any under- or over-receipt of cash (in comparison with the receivable recorded) is adjusted against revenue.

A business sold goods to a customer on credit at a list price of $240. Early settlement discount of 4% was offered to the customer for payment within 7 days of invoice date.

If the customer is expected to take advantage of the settlement discount offered, the revenue and receivable will be recorded as: $240 × 96% = $230.40.

If the customer is not expected to take advantage of the settlement discount offered, the revenue and receivable will be recorded as $240.

Sales tax

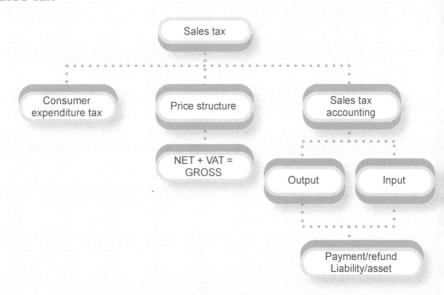

- Sales tax is levied at the point of sale of a good or service, by way of a percentage add-on to the pre-tax (net) selling price. The rate varies from country to country, but the standard rate in the UK is 20%. Please be aware that ACCA could ask questions using any rate they choose. You therefore need to be able to manipulate the calculation using a variety of % rates.
- The business merely collects sales tax on behalf of the tax authorities. At no time does the sales tax belong to the business. At regular intervals the business either pays sales tax to, or has sales tax repaid by, the tax authorities.
- The **profit is based on the net of sales tax figures.**

Assuming a sales tax rate of 20%:

Using the sales tax **exclusive** figure (**net**)	Using the sales tax **inclusive** figure (**gross**)
• Sales tax = net × 20/120	• sales tax = gross × 20/120.
• To calculate the gross figure: gross = net × 120%.	• To calculate the net figure: net = gross × 100/120.

Credit sales and sales tax

Step 1: The double entry required for a credit sale with sales tax is:

Debit	Receivables (gross amount)	x
Credit	Sales (net amount)	x
Credit	Sales tax account (tax)	x

Step 2: When the customer pays the debt, the total invoice amount is recorded in the bank account. The sales tax account is not affected.

Debit	Bank	x
Credit	Receivables	x

Credit purchases and sales tax

Step 1: The double entry required for a credit purchase with sales tax is

Debit	Purchases/expense (net amount)	x
Debit	Sales tax account (tax)	x
Credit	Payables	x

Step 2: When the business pays the debt to the supplier, the total invoice amount is paid from the bank account. The sales tax account is not affected.

Debit	Payables	x
Credit	Bank	x

Sales tax account			
Bal b/d (refund due)	x	Bal b/d (amount due)	x
Bank (payment made for opening amount due)	x	Bank (refund received)	x
Purchases/expenses	x	Sales	x
Bal c/d (amount due)	x	Bal c/d (refund due)	x
	x		x
Bal b/d (refund due)	x	Bal b/d (amount due)	x

4

Inventory

In this chapter

- Accounting for inventory.
- Valuation of inventory.
- IAS 2 requirements.
- Disclosure note.

Inventory is most likely to be examined regarding valuation and adjustment in the financial statements. You also need to be aware of the accounting concepts that are relevant regarding inventory.

Accounting for inventory

Opening inventory is found in the ledger accounts and therefore appears in the trial balance.

It is **transferred to the statement of profit or loss and other comprehensive income** at the end of the accounting period.

	\$	\$
Sales revenue		X
Opening inventory	X	
Purchases	X	
Less: Closing inventory	(X)	
Cost of sales		(X)
Gross profit		X

Closing inventory is obtained by counting the inventory at the period end. It does **not** appear **in the trial balance** – you will find it in the additional information given at the end of a question. It is entered in the ledger accounts at the end of the year. It **appears in both the statement of profit or loss and other comprehensive income and in the statement of financial position** as a current asset.

It is included via the following journal:

Dr Closing Inventory – SFP   x

Cr Closing Inventory – P&L   x

Valuation of inventory

Value inventory at the 'lower of cost and net realisable value (NRV)' (IAS 2, para 9):

This comparison must be made item by item, not on the total inventory value. It may be acceptable to consider groups of items together if all are worth less than cost.

Cost	Net realisable value
Includes all the expenditure incurred in bringing the product or service to its present location and condition: • cost of **purchase** – material costs, import duties, freight • cost of **conversion** – **direct costs** e.g. of materials and **production overheads** e.g. factory light and heat.	The revenue (sales proceeds) expected to be earned in the future when the goods are sold, less any further costs (including selling costs) that need to be incurred.

Concepts relevant to the valuation of inventory

Matching concept	Justifies the carrying forward of unsold inventory, to ensure that only the inventory which has actually been sold is 'matched' with the sales revenue generated.
Prudence concept	Requires a business to recognise a loss as soon as it is realised that the cost of the inventory will not be recovered by a subsequent sale.

IAS 2 requirements

- IAS 2 requires unit cost to be used where possible. Unit cost is the actual cost of purchasing identifiable units of inventory. This method is used where inventory items are of high value and individually distinguishable (e.g. jewellery and art).

- Otherwise:
  - FIFO or weighted average cost are benchmark treatments.
  - FIFO (first in first out) assumes that items of Inventory received are the first items to be sold.
  - Weighted average cost can be calculated either on either a periodic basis or on a continuous basis.
  - Periodic AVCO – calculated at the end of the accounting period based upon opening inventory plus purchases made during the accounting period.
  - Continuous AVCO – recalculated each time there is a purchase during the accounting period.

Disclosure note

Inventories are valued at the lower of cost and net realisable value.

They will be analysed as follows in the notes to the accounts.

	20XX
	£000
Raw materials and consumables	X
Work in progress	X
Finished goods and goods for resale	X
	X

5

Non-current assets

In this chapter

- Asset v expense.
- Accounting for depreciation.
- Methods of depreciation.
- Sale of non-current assets.
- Revaluation of non-current assets.
- Double entry for revaluation.
- Double entry for excess depreciation.
- IAS 16 Property, Plant and Equipment.
- Note detailing movements in property, plant and equipment.
- IAS 38 Intangible Assets.

There will always be questions on this topic. You will be required to identify asset expenditure and expense items, calculate depreciation charges, profit/losses on disposals of non-current assets and revaluation adjustments.

Asset v expense

Asset expenditure	Expenses
Costs of acquiring a non-current asset, including legal fees, delivery and installation costs. Improvements to non-current assets.	Day-to-day running costs such as maintenance, repairs, replacement parts, redecoration.
Appears as an **asset** on the **statement of financial position**.	Written off as an **expense** in the **statement of profit or loss and other comprehensive income**.

Matching concept requires revenue and costs to be matched. Therefore the cost of a non-current asset should be written off as an expense in the accounting periods expected to benefit from its use.

Depreciation is the systematic allocation of the depreciable amount of a non-current asset over its useful life. (Depreciable amount = carrying amount less residual value).

Factors to be taken into account in assessing depreciation = cost or valuation of asset, expected useful economic life to the business and estimated residual value at end of life.

Accounting for depreciation

On acquisition of non-current asset:

Debit	Credit	With
Non-current asset – cost	Cash/Supplier	Cost of the asset

At the end of each year make the adjustment for depreciation:

Debit	Credit	With
Depreciation expense account – charge to P&L	Non-current asset – accumulated depreciation	Depreciation charge

Methods of depreciation

Straight line method

% on cost

or; $\dfrac{\text{Cost} - \text{Residual Value}}{\text{Useful economic life}}$

Reducing balance method

This method results in higher depreciation charges in earlier years. A percentage is applied to cost in the first period and to the net carrying amount in subsequent years.

Take care! If assets have been sold during the year, the accumulated depreciation b/f must be reduced by the accumulated depreciation on the disposals, before the current year's charge is calculated.

Sale of non-current assets

	Debit	Credit	With
1	Disposals account	Non-current asset – cost account	Original cost of asset
2	Non-current asset – accumulated depreciation account	Disposals account	Accumulated depreciation up to the date of disposal
3(a)	Cash/bank	Disposals account	Proceeds of sale
3(b)	Non-current asset – cost	Disposals account	Trade-in value of old asset if part-exchanged for new asset
4(a)	Disposals account	Profit or loss – income	Profit on sale
4(b)	Profit or loss – expense	Disposals account	Loss on sale

	Disposals a/c				
1	Non-current asset – Cost	X	2	Accumulated Depreciation	X
			3(a)	Cash/Bank	X
			3(b)	Non-current asset	X
4(a)	P&L – profit on sale	X	4(b)	P&L – loss on sale	X
		X			X

Revaluation of non-current assets

- **Reason for revaluation**: to reflect the current worth of assets on the statement of financial position.

- The difference (usually a surplus) between the revalued amount and the previous net book value is recognised as an item of **other comprehensive income** and is credited to a **revaluation surplus** within equity in the SFP.

- **Depreciation**

  - charged on original cost until the date of the revaluation

  - at time of revaluation, accumulated depreciation on original cost is transferred to the revaluation surplus

  - after revaluation, is based on the revalued amount and spread over the asset's remaining useful economic life. The new depreciation charge will therefore be higher than previously

  - provision for accumulated depreciation at the year end only consists of the depreciation charged on the revalued amount

  - remember that the entity may also have a policy of making an annual transfer of excess depreciation from revaluation surplus to retained earning within the SOCIE. If this is the case, you will be told in the exam question.

Double entry for revaluation

Debit	Credit	With
Non – current asset	Revaluation surplus	Increase in cost
Accumulated depreciation	Revaluation surplus	Removal of accumulated depreciation up to date of revaluation

Double entry for excess depreciation

Debit	Credit	With
Revaluation surplus	Retained earnings	Excess depreciation for the year

IAS 16 Property, Plant and Equipment

Measurement

The initial measurement of the value of a tangible non-current asset should be cost. This includes **directly attributable costs** of 'bringing the asset to the location and condition necessary for it to be capable of operating in the manner intended by management'.

Depreciation

Each part of an asset with a cost that is significant in relation to the total cost of the asset must be **depreciated separately**. Land normally has an unlimited life and so does not require depreciation, but buildings should be depreciated.

Review of residual value, useful life and depreciation method

These should be reviewed at least **each financial year end** and changed if expectations differ from previous estimates or if the depreciation methods used no longer reflect the rate of usage of the asset. Any **changes** should be **accounted for as a change in accounting estimate in accordance with IAS 8**.

Derecognition

Derecognise an asset on disposal or when no future economic benefits are expected from its use. The gain or loss arising from the derecognition of an asset is the difference between its carrying amount and the net disposal proceeds. Recognise in the statement of comprehensive income.

Note detailing movements in property, plant and equipment

	Land & buildings	Plant & machinery	Fixtures & fittings	Motor vehicles	Total
	$m	$m	$m	$m	$m
Cost:					
Beginning of year	x	x	x	x	x
Additions	x	x	x	x	x
Disposals	(x)	(x)	(x)	(x)	(x)
End of year	x	x	x	x	x
Depreciation:					
Beginning of year	x	x	x	x	x
Charged during year	x	x	x	x	x
Disposals	(x)	(x)	(x)	(x)	(x)
End of year	x	x	x	x	x
Carrying amount:					
Beginning of year	x	x	x	x	x
End of year	x	x	x	x	x

IAS 38 Intangible Assets

Many entities invest significant amounts with the intention of obtaining future value on areas such as:

- scientific/technical knowledge
- design of new processes and systems
- licences and quotas
- intellectual property, e.g. patents and copyrights
- market knowledge, e.g. customer lists, relationships and loyalty
- trademarks

All these expenses may result in future benefits to the entity, but not all can be recognised as assets.

Objective of IAS 38 Intangible assets

The objective of IAS 38 is to prescribe the specific criteria that must be met before an intangible asset can be recognised in the accounts.

An intangible asset '**is an identifiable non-monetary asset without physical substance**' (IAS 38, para 8).

To meet the definition the asset must be identifiable, ie. separable from the rest of the business or arising from legal rights.

It must also meet the normal definition of the asset:

- controlled by the entity as a result of past events (normally by enforceable legal rights)
- a resource from which future economic benefits are expected to flow (either from from revenue or cost saving).

Recognition

To be recognised in the financial statements, an intangible asset must:

- meet the definition of an intangible asset, and
- meet the recognition criteria of the framework:
  - it is probable that future economic benefits attributable to the asset will flow to the entity
  - the cost of the asset can be measured reliably
  - If these criteria are met, the asset should be initially recognised at cost.

Disclosure

The notes to the accounts will detail the total intangible non-curret assets in the statement of financial position at net book value.

The main area for examination in this standard is that of Research and Development

Research – Definition	Recognition
'Original and planned investigation undertaken with the prospect of gaining new scientific or technical knowledge and understanding' (IAS 38, para 8).	Expenditure on research should be recognised as an **expense** in the period in which it is incurred.

Development – Definition	Recognition
'The application of research findings or other knowledge to a plan or design for the production of new or substantially improved materials, devices, products, processes, systems or services before the start of commercial production or use' (IAS 38, para 9).	Recognise as an **intangible asset**, if and only if all the following can be demonstrated:
	• the **technical feasibility** of completing the development
The cost of an internally generated development work	• the **intention** of the entity to **complete** the development
The sum of all directly attributable costs to create the asset and make it ready for use in the manner intended by management. E.g.	• the **ability** of the entity to **use or sell** the item
• costs of materials, services and labour	• how the intangible asset will generate future **economic benefits**
• fees to register a legal right.	• the **availability** of adequate technical, financial and other **resources to complete** the asset
Only expenditure incurred from the time that the intangible asset was recognised is included. Expenditure incurred during the research phase cannot be re-classified from an expense to an intangible asset.	• the **ability to measure reliably** expenditure on the intangible asset during its development.
	When the requirements can all be demonstrated, **subsequent** expenditure should be classified as an intangible asset.

Amortisation

Capitalised development costs must be **amortised** once commercial exploitation begins. The **method** should reflect the pattern in which the asset's economic benefits are consumed by the entity. If that pattern cannot be determined reliably, the straight-line method should be used.

6

Receivables, payables and provisions

In this chapter

- Accrued and prepaid expenses and income.
- Trade receivables in the general ledger.
- Irrecoverable debts.
- Allowance for receivables.
- Trade payables in the general ledger.
- Provisions, contingent liabilities and contingent assets: IAS 37.

You must understand the accounting principles and requirements of reporting standards within this chapter. You must also be able to apply them to the various practical situations set in a question.

Accrued and prepaid expenses and income

Accrued expenditure

This arises when the expenditure relating to the period has not been paid.

The amount owing at the end of the period is adjusted as follows:

Dr Expense (P&L) Cr Accrued expenditure (SFP liability)

In an ongoing business there could be an opening and a closing accrual.

Accrued expenditure – Proforma expense T account

Expense			
		Bal b/d (opening accrued expense)	X
Bank (total paid during the year)	X	SP&L (total expense for the year)	X
Bal c/d (closing accrued expense)	X		
	X		X
		Bal b/d (opening accrued expense)	X

Prepaid expenditure

This arises when the expenditure relating to the period has been paid in advance.

The amount prepaid at the end of the period is adjusted as follows:

Dr Prepayment (SFP asset) Cr Expense

In an ongoing business there could be an opening and a closing prepayment.

Prepaid expenditure – Proforma expense T account

Expense			
Bal b/d (opening prepaid expense)	X		
Bank (total paid during the year)	X	SP&L	
		(total expense for the year)	X
		Bal c/d (closing prepaid expense)	X
	X		X
Bal b/d (opening prepaid expense)	X		

Prepaid income

Prepaid income arises when the income has been received in the period but relates to the next accounting period.

The prepaid income will be accounted for as follows:

    Dr Income (P&L) Cr Prepaid/ deferred income (SFP)

Accrued income

Accrued income arises when the income has been earned in the period but has not been received.

The accrued income will be accounted for as follows:

    Dr Accrued income (SFP) Cr Income (P&L)

Trade receivables in the general ledger

The receivables account may contain any of the following entries:

Trade receivables			
	$		$
Balance b/f	X	Sales returns	X
Credit sales	X	Cash at bank	X
Bank – dishonoured cheques	X	Irrecoverable debts	X
Bank – refunds of credit balances	X	Trade payables – contra	X
Interest charged on overdue accounts	X	Balance c/f	X
	X		X
Balance b/f	X		

Irrecoverable debts

If a debt is considered to be uncollectible, it should be written off.

To write off an **irrecoverable** debt	If an **irrecoverable** debt is recovered
Dr irrecoverable debts expense account Cr Receivables	Dr Bank Cr irrecoverable debts recovered account

Total irrecoverable debts = **expense** in **SP&L**

Irrecoverable debts **do not appear** in the **statement of financial position** as they have already been deducted from the figure of receivables.

Allowance for receivables

Where a customer is known to be in financial difficulties and therefore the amount owing may not be recoverable, an allowance can be created. The debt remains in the ledger accounts, but the allowance is deducted from the figure of receivables in the statement of financial position.

- Dr Irrecoverable debts expense account
- Cr Allowance for receivables account

In the following period if there is a decrease in the allowance the double entry will be as follows:

- Dr Allowance for receivables account
- Cr Irrecoverable debts expense account

Format of the allowance for receivables account

Allowance for receivables

		Bal b/d (opening allowance)	X
SP&L (decrease in allowance)	X	SP&L (increase in allowance)	X
Bal c/d (closing allowance)	X		
	X		X

Statement of financial position

The **total** allowance is deducted from the figure of receivables.

You will be required to calculate any of the figures regarding the irrecoverable debts or allowance for receivables figure.

	20X6	20X7
	$	$
Current assets:		
Receivables (less irrecoverable debts written off)	x	x
Less:		
Allowance for receivables	x	x
	x	x

Statement of profit or loss and other comprehensive income

Only the **change** in the allowance for receivables is included in the statement of profit or loss, normally within the irrecoverable debts expense account. An increase in the allowance is treated as an expense. A reduction in the allowance is treated as either income or a negative expense.

Trade payables in the general ledger

The trade payables' general ledger account may include any of the following entries:

Trade payables

Cash at bank	X	Balance b/f	X
Purchases returns	X	Credit purchases	X
Early settlement discounts received	X	Interest on overdue accounts	X
Contra with trade receivables	X		
Balance c/f	X		
	X		X
		Balance b/f	X

Provisions, contingent liabilities and contingent assets: IAS 37

A provision is '**a liability of uncertain timing and/or amount**' (IAS 37, para 10).

A provision can be recognised only when three criteria have been complied with:

- there is an obligation (legal or constructive) arising from a past transaction or event,
- it is probable that there will be a future outflow of economic benefits, and
- the amount can be reliably estimated
- **Treatment** – A provision should be recognised in the financial statements.

Contingent Asset: IAS 37

A contingent asset is a possible asset that arises from past events, and whose existence will be confirmed only by the occurrence or non-occurrence of one or more uncertain future events that are not wholly within the company's control.

Treatment – A contingent asset should not be recognised in the financial statements because this may result in the recognition of income that may never be realised.

The **inflow** of economic benefits is **virtually certain**	The **inflow** of economic benefits is **probable**, but not certain	The **inflow** is **not probable**
The asset is not a contingent asset	Do **not** recognise the asset	Do **not** recognise
Recognise the asset (and any associated income)	Disclose: • a brief description of the nature of the asset, and • where practicable, an estimate of its financial effect	No disclosure required

Contingent liabilities: IAS 37

Definition	Treatment

Either:
 	
 • a **possible obligation** that arises from past events and whose existence will be **confirmed only by** the occurrence or non-occurrence of one or more **uncertain future events** that are not wholly within the company's control, or
 	
 • a **present obligation** arising out of past events that is not recognised as a provision because:
 	
    – it is not probable that an outflow of 'resources embodying economic benefits' will be required to settle the obligation, or
 	
    – the amount of the obligation cannot be measured with sufficient reliability.
	If obligation is probable (over **50% likelihood**) → make a **provision** (i.e. treat as an expense in the P&L and a liability in the SOFP).
	
	 If probability is **less than 50% = contingent liability.**
	
	 • **Not recognised as a liability** in the SFP, nor as an expense in measuring profit or loss.
	
	 • **Disclose** in the notes for each class:
	
	    – the nature of the contingent liability, and
	
	    – where possible, an estimate of its financial effect and of the uncertainties relating to the amount of timing of any outflow.
	
	 If probability is very low, contingent liability = '**remote**'. Do not disclose at all.

7

Capital structure and finance costs

In this chapter

- Types of capital.
- Share capital – terminology.
- Accounting for share issues.
- Equity reserves.

Topics contained in this chapter will appear
regularly in the examination. You must learn
the terminology, specific for companies such
as different types of share capital, equity
reserves, bonus/rights issues.

Types of capital

	Loan capital	Share capital
Definition	A loan note (debenture) is a document issued by a company containing an acknowledgment of its indebtedness.	A share is the interest of a shareholder in a company measured by a sum of money.
Voting rights	A creditor of the company, therefore no voting rights.	A member (owner) of the company, therefore voting rights depending on class of shares.
Income	Contractual right to interest irrespective of availability of profits.	Dividends depend on availability of profits.
Liquidation	Preferential right to repayment.	Receive repayment after creditors, but can participate in surplus assets.

	Preference shares	Ordinary shares (equity)
Voting rights	None, or restricted.	Full.
Dividend rights	Fixed dividend paid in priority to other dividends, usually cumulative.	Paid after preference dividend. Not fixed.
Surplus on winding up	Prior return of capital, but cannot participate in any surplus.	Entitled to share surplus assets after repayment of preference shares.

Share capital – terminology

Authorised capital	The **maximum** number of shares a company can issue.
Issued capital	The number of shares actually issued. It is this figure that appears on the statement of financial position.
Nominal value	Shares usually have a **face value**. Also known as a par or nominal value. This is not necessarily the price at which the shares were originally issued. The nominal value is usually used when calculating dividends.
Market value	The market value of a share is determined by the value of the business. It is quoted on the stock exchange if the company is listed. It has no relevance to the company's financial statements.
Bonus issues	Some of the company's equity reserves are used to issue fully paid shares to existing shareholders in proportion to their shareholdings. **Doesn't raise any new funds**. Often carried out if the market price per share is very high. It results in a fall in the market price as the value of the company is divided between more shares.
Rights issues	New shares offered to existing shareholders in proportion to their shareholdings. Raises new funds. Shares usually offered at discount to current market value (but not at discount to nominal value). Therefore greater chance of success compared with share issue to the public.

Accounting for share issues

	Debit	Credit
Issue of shares at a premium for cash (including rights issues)	Cash/Bank	Share capital (nominal value)
		Share premium (premium)
Bonus issue ('free' issue)	Equity reserves	Share account

Equity reserves

Share capital + equity reserves = equity of the company = carrying amount of the net assets of the company.

Capital reserves	Revenue reserves
Can't be used for distributions to shareholders, but can be used for bonus issues. Main examples are as follows. **Share premium**: the excess of the issue price of a share over its nominal value. **Revaluation surplus**: arises when an increase in the value of a non-current asset is recognised. It represents the excess of the new value over the previous book value (carrying amount).	**Can be distributed**. Main examples: • **Accumulated profit:** total profit made by the company since it was formed, minus dividends paid. • **Inventory** replacement reserve: same principle. • **General reserve:** no specific purpose for the reserve. Although legally the reserve can be distributed as a dividend, the directors are indicating that it is not available for distribution.

8

Reconciliations

In this chapter

- Bank reconciliations.
- Supplier statement reconciliations.

Topics contained in this chapter will appear regularly in the examination. You must understand how to perform a bank reconciliation and a supplier statement reconciliation.

Bank reconciliations

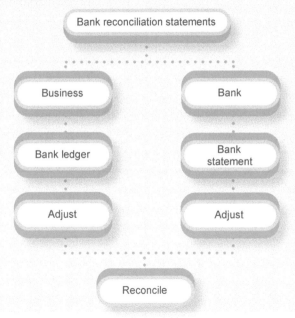

Bank ledger – Records all of the business's transactions with the bank.	=	**Bank statement** – Issued by the bank. Shows all the bank's transactions with the business.
Items in bank statement but not bank ledger: • bank charges • bank interest paid or received • standing orders and direct debits • credit transfers (receipts paid direct into bank) • dishonoured cheques.		Items in bank ledger but not bank statement: • unpresented cheques (cheques issued by the business not yet presented to the bank) • deposits which have not yet cleared (also known as outstanding lodgements) • bank errors. (Unpresented cheques and outstanding deposits are examples of timing differences.)
Write up these items in the bank ledger.		Produce a bank reconciliation statement.

Bank reconciliation statement

	£
Balance per bank statement	X/(X)
Bank error	X/(X)
	X
Unpresented cheques	(X)
Outstanding deposits	X
Balance per corrected bank ledger	X(X)

Supplier statement reconciliations

Supplier statement reconciliations

Business	Supplier
Payable ledger account	Supplier statement
Adjust for: • invoice not yet recorded • credit note not yet recorded • errors recording transactions	Adjust for: • payment not recorded • discount received not recorded • errors on supplier statement

Reconcile

9

Trial balance and errors

In this chapter

- The journal.
- Errors not revealed by the trial balance.
- Errors revealed by the trial balance in a manual system.
- The suspense account.

The topics in this chapter will always appear in the exam.

Ensure that you remember which errors do not affect the trial balance – they still need to be adjusted.

In a computerised accounting system, errors such as recording an unequal value of debits and credits would not be possible. Many human errors, such as arithmetic errors calculating ledger account balances, or when extracting and recording ledger account balances would not occur, whereas they could occur in a manual accounting system.

The journal

The journal: a record of non-routine transactions and ledger entries, such as:

- adjustments to the final accounts
- acquisitions and disposals of non-current assets
- correction of errors.

Journal entry: sets out a bookkeeping double entry that is to be made.

Date	Details	Ledger folio	Dr	Cr
			$	$
20X9				
6 Feb	Van account	V1	x	
	Motor expenses account	M3		x

Purchase of van incorrectly debited to motor expenses.

The narrative line should give a brief explanation of the entry.

Errors not revealed by the trial balance

Error of omission	• **No entry** for a transaction has been made at all.
Error of commission	• An amount has been correctly posted, but to the **wrong account**. E.g. a sale on credit to G Brown has been posted to the account of J Brown.
Error of principle	• An item is posted to the **wrong type of account**. E.g. a new tyre for a van has been posted to the Van account (non-current asset) rather than to the Motor Repairs account (expense).
Error of original entry	• An **incorrect amount** is posted to both the accounts in question.
Compensating error	• Two or more **errors cancel out each other**. They are difficult to locate and fortunately tend not to occur frequently.
Reversal of entries	• The correct amounts have been posted to the correct accounts, but on the **wrong side**.
Transposition errors	• E.g. $527 is recorded as $725. (The difference the error creates is always divisible by 9.) Not revealed by the trial balance if the same figure has been used on both sides of the double entry.

Errors revealed by the trial balance in a manual system

- **Single sided entry** – Only one side of the double entry has been made, e.g. the debit, but not the credit.
- Debit and credit entries have been made, but using **different figures**.
- **Both entries** have been made on the **same side**.
- An individual account has been **miscast** (i.e. added up incorrectly).
- An opening balance has not been brought down.
- **Extraction error** – the balance in the trial balance is different from the balance in the account.

The suspense account

A **suspense account** is an account in which debits or credits are held temporarily until sufficient information is available for them to be posted to the correct accounts.

Why are suspense accounts created?

- Book-keeping uncertainty: where it is not clear to a book-keeper where to post one side of an entry, it may be debited or credited to a suspense account.

Adjustments to the net profit

The net profit will need to be adjusted if:

- an entry affects an account included within the statement of comprehensive income
- an entry affects a non-current asset account, as you may need to adjust the depreciation charge.

Exam focus

Questions may be set which require you to account for irrecoverable debts and to account for a change in the allowance for receivables.

Other questions may require you to record transactions that appear in the receivables account, such as recording contra entries with the payables account.

10

Preparing basic financial statements

In this chapter

- From trial balance to financial statements.
- Components of financial statements.
- Statement of financial position.
- Statement of profit or loss and other comprehensive income.
- Statement of changes in equity.
- Other comprehensive income.
- Revenue from contracts with customers IFRS 15.
- Events after the reporting period IAS 10.

The statement of financial position and statements of profit or loss and other comprehensive income shown in this chapter are similar to those shown in earlier chapters. However, published accounts are **required** to use the formats shown below.

From trial balance to financial statements

Some of the trial balance (TB) figures may need to be adjusted before going into the financial statements. The table below shows the most common adjustments. **Read the question carefully** as the examiner may give you different information from what you would usually expect to see.

Inventory	TB figure = opening inventory. Notes under TB give closing inventory.
Depreciation	TB figure = accumulated depreciation b/f from previous year. Deduct the accumulated depreciation charged on any assets sold during the year. Add the current year's depreciation charge.
Non-current assets	TB figure = cost b/f from the previous year. Deduct the cost of any assets sold during the year. Add the current year's acquisitions.
Prepayments	TB figures of expenses = amounts paid during the year. Deduct any prepayments (i.e. amounts paid, but which relate to next year's accounts) to get statement of comprehensive income figure. Show prepayments as current asset in statement of financial position.
Accruals	TB figures of expenses = amounts paid during the year. Add accruals (i.e. amounts owing) at the year end to get SP&L figure. Show accruals as current liability in SOFP.
Irrecoverable debts	TB figure = debts written off (i.e. already deducted from figure of receivables). Show as an expense in the SP&L. (To write off any irrecoverable debts not shown in the TB, show as an expense in the P&L and also deduct from the TB figure of receivables.)
Allowance for receivables	TB figure = b/f from previous year. P&L only shows the change to the allowance (i.e. increase = expense, reduction = income/negative expense). Deduct closing provision (i.e. b/f + increase/- reduction) from receivables in SOFP.

Components of financial statements

IAS 1 Presentation of Financial Statements sets out the information that must be presented in all 'general purpose' financial statements.

A complete set of financial statements should include:

- a **statement of financial position**
- a **statement of statement of profit or loss and other comprehensive income**
- a **statement of changes in equity**, showing either:
  - all changes in equity, or
  - changes in equity other than those arising from transactions with the shareholders (for example, money raised from share issues or dividend distributions)

- a **statement of cash flows** (dealt with in the next chapter)
- **notes** to these statements, consisting of a summary of the accounting policies used by the company and other explanatory notes (dealt with in the appropriate chapters).

Comparative information for the previous accounting period should be disclosed, unless an IFRS permits or requires otherwise.

Statement of financial position

Statement of financial position of ABC Company
as at 31 December 20XX

Assets	$m	$m
Non-current assets		
Property, plant and equipment	x	
Intangible assets	x	
Investments	x	
	___	x
Current assets		
Inventories	x	
Trade and other receivables	x	
Cash	x	
	___	
		x
Total assets		x

→ Present all assets and liabilities in order of liquidity.

→ Present non-current assets separately from current assets.

→ Asset = current if:
   – part of operating cycle, or
   – held for trading purposes, or
   – expected to be realised within 12 months of BS date, or
   – cash or a cash equivalent.

Equity and liabilities	$m	$m	
Equity			
Issued capital	x		
Equity reserves		x	
Retained earnings	x		→ Sum of the accumulated profits and losses
	────	x	
Non-current liabilities			
Long-term loans		x	
Current liabilities			→ Liability = current if:
Trade and other payables	x		– expected to be settled in the normal course of the operating cycle of the entity, or
Short-term borrowings (bank overdraft)	x		– held primarily for the purpose of being traded, or
Tax	x		– due to be settled within 12 months of the reporting date, or
	────	x	– no unconditional right to defer settlement to at least 12 months after the reporting date.
Total equity and liabilities		x	

Statement of profit or loss and other comprehensive income

ABC Company
Statement of profit or loss and other
comprehensive income for the year ended 31 December 20XX

	$m
Revenue	x
Cost of sales	x
	x
Other income	(x)
Distribution costs	(x)
Administrative expenses	(x)
	x
Finance costs	(x)
Profit before tax	x
Tax expense	(x)
Profit for the period	x
Other Comprehensive income:	
Revaluation surplus/(loss) in the year	x/(x)
Total Comprehensive Income	x

→ Analysis of expenses may be on the face of the SP&L or in the notes.

Statement of changes in equity

This shows all of the changes which have affected the various classes of equity (previously referred to as share capital and equity reserves).

ABC Company
Statement of changes in equity for the year ended 31 December 20XX

	Share capital $000	Share premium $000	Revaluation surplus $000	Retained earnings $000	Total $000
Balance at 31 December Year 1	x	x	x	x	x
Change in accounting policy	–	–	–	(x)	(x)
Re-stated balance	x	x	x	x	x
Changes in equity for Year 2					
Surplus on revaluation of properties			x		x
Deficit on revaluation of properties			(x)		(x)
Net gains and losses not recognised in the SOCI			x		x
Net profit for the period			–	x	x
Dividends paid				(x)	(x)
Issue of share capital	x	x	–	–	x
Balance at 31 December Year 2	x	x	x	x	x

Other comprehensive income

IAS 1 requires that a distinction is made between items of profit or loss and items of other comprehensive income in the statement of profit or loss and other comprehensive income.

These two elements can be presented as one combined statement, dealing first with profit or loss and then dealing with other comprehensive income as illustrated earlier.

Alternatively, they can be shown as two separate statements.

If there are no items of other comprehensive income in the year, it is sufficient to make a disclosure statement to that effect immediately below the statement of profit or loss.

XYZ Company
Statement of other comprehensive income for the year ended 31 December Year 2

	$000
Profit for the year	x
Other comprehensive income:	
Surplus on revaluation of properties	x
Deficit on revaluation of properties	(x)
Total comprehensive income for the year	x

Revenue from contracts with customers IFRS 15

IFRS 15

Step 1 – Identify the contract

Step 2 – Identify the separate performance obligations within the contracts

Step 3 – Determine the transaction price

Step 4 – Allocate the transaction price to the performance obligations in the contract

Step 5 – Recognise revenue when (or as) a performance obligation is satisfied

If an obligation is satisfied at a point in time, recognise revenue at point the obligation is satisfied. This is likely to apply to the sale of goods.

If an obligation is satisfied over a period of time, recognise revenue over period of time that the obligation is satisfied. This is likely to apply to the provision of services.

If necessary, identify separate performance obligations and recognise revenue as each obligation is satisfied. Consider, for example, the sale of a computer plus a 12-month technical support agreement. Revenue relating to the sale of the computer can be recognised when control is transferred to the purchaser (i.e. at a point in time) and revenue on the technical support agreement can be recognised over the support period (i.e. over a period of time).

One step in the process to determine revenue is the requirement to determine the transaction price, including the probability of receiving variable consideration. This was considered in chapter 3 when dealing with settlement discounts available to customers.

Events after the reporting period: IAS 10

'An event, favourable or unfavourable, that happens after the reporting period but before the financial statements are authorised for issue' (IAS 10, para 3). (An entity should disclose when the financial statements were authorised for issue, and who gave the authorisation.)

Adjusting events	Non-adjusting events
Provide evidence of a condition that existed at the reporting date.	Indicate a condition that arose after the end of the reporting period.
The financial statements should be **adjusted** to reflect these events. E.g.: • after the reporting period, the company learns that it must make a payment to settle a court case • information received after the reporting period that an asset's value was impaired at the end of the reporting period (e.g. a customer goes out of business) • establishing after the reporting period the amount of a bonus payment to employees, which the company has an obligation to make.	The financial statements should not be adjusted, but for each material category disclose: • the **nature** of the event, and • an **estimate of its financial effect**, or a statement that such an estimate cannot be made. Examples requiring disclosure: • a major acquisition or the disposal of a major part of the business after the reporting period • major purchases of assets or the destruction of a major asset • an issue of shares for cash after the reporting period. **Dividends** declared after the reporting period, but before the financial statements are approved should not be recognised as a liability in the end-of-year statement of financial position (but disclose in the notes per IAS 1).

11

Incomplete records

In this chapter

- Incomplete records – overview.
- Margin v mark up.
- Finding missing information.

This topic is a popular area in the exams. You should be able to use ledger accounts and ratios to determine missing figures.

Incomplete records – overview

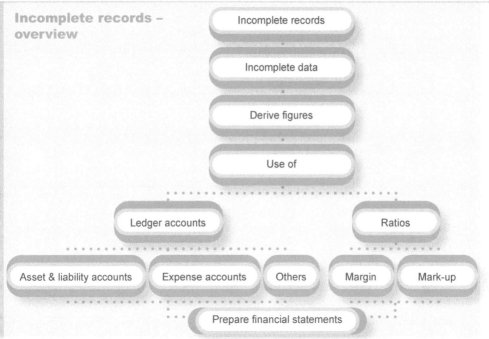

Incomplete records

Incomplete data

Derive figures

Use of

Ledger accounts

Ratios

Asset & liability accounts

Expense accounts

Others

Margin

Mark-up

Prepare financial statements

Margin v mark-up

With **gross profit margin** the percentage of profit is given by reference to **sales revenue**.

Gross profit percentage or profit margin =

$$\frac{\text{Gross profit}}{\text{Sales revenue}} \times 100$$

Margin × sales = Gross profit

Thus if we know that sales revenue totals $8,000 and the gross profit percentage is 25%, the following can be deduced:

	$	%
Sales revenue	8,000 (given)	100
Less: Cost of sales	6,000	75
Gross profit	2,000	25 (given)

The gross profit is calculated as follows:
25% × $8,000 = £2,000

All the other items are derived as balancing items.

With **gross profit mark-up** the percentage of profit is given by reference to **cost of sales.**

Gross profit mark-up percentage =

$$\frac{\text{Gross profit}}{\text{Cost of sales}} \times 100$$

Mark-up × cost of sales = Gross profit

Thus if we know that cost of sales is $6,000 and the mark-up is one third, we can set out the following:

	$	Ratio
Sales revenue	8,000	4
Cost of sales	6,000 (given)	3
Gross profit	2,000	1

The gross profit is calculated as follows:
1/3 × $6,000 = $2,000

Exam trick

An exam question will often provide you with margin and cost of sales or mark-up and sales. You will then be required to calculate the remaining figures in the trading account. This can be done using the following 'relationship' columns:

Margin 25%		Mark-up 25%	
Sales	2. 100%	Sales	3. 100+ratio
Cost of sales	3. 100-ratio	Cost of sales	2. 100%
Gross profit	1. Ratio	Gross profit	1. Ratio

Finding missing information

What's missing?	Where will I find it?
Sales, cost of sales or closing inventory	• Draft the statement of profit or loss and other comprehensive income down as far as the figure of gross profit and insert all the relevant figures from the question.
	• Use the gross profit margin/mark-up formula, as appropriate, to calculate the missing figure of sales/cost of sales.
	• Work backwards to ascertain any missing figures, e.g. closing inventory.

What's missing?	Where will I find it?
Credit sales or money received from customers	The receivables account. If you're missing more than one figure, it may be necessary to complete some other working first, e.g.: • balance the cash account to find the amount of cash received, or • use the gross profit margin/mark-up formula to find the sales figure.

Receivables account

	$		$
Opening receivables b/d	X	Cash received	X
Credit sales	X	Closing receivables c/d	X
	X		X

There may be other items that may need to be incorporated into the above working, such as a contra with the payables account and sales returns.

What's missing?	Where will I find it?
Credit purchases or money paid to suppliers	The payables account.
	If you're missing more than one figure, it may be necessary to complete some other working first, e.g.:
	• balance the cash account to find the amount of cash paid, or
	• use the gross profit margin/mark-up formula to find the purchases figure.

Payables account

	$		$
Cash	X	Opening trade payables b/d	X
Bank	X	Purchases	X
Closing trade payables c/d	X		
	X		X

There may be other items that may need to be incorporated into the above working, such as a contra with the receivables account, discount received and purchases returns.

What's missing?	Where will I find it?
Drawings, cash sales, cash purchases, stolen cash	The cash and/or bank account.
	If you're missing more than one figure, it may be necessary to complete some other working first, e.g.: balance the receivables account to find the amount of cash received from customers.

Cash/Bank

	$		$
Balance b/d	X	Cash expenses/purchases	X
Cash sales	X	Drawings	X
		Payments to credit suppliers	X
Receipts from credit customers	X	Balance c/d	X
	X		X

What's missing?	Where will I find it?
Opening capital	The opening capital account balance can be calculated as a balancing figure (capital = assets – liabilities). Show your workings in the form of a trial balance or a basic statement of financial position.

	Dr	Cr
	$	$
Non-current assets	X	
Bank	X	
Cash	X	
Receivables	X	
Trade payables		X
Accruals		X
Inventory	X	
	A	B

Net assets = opening capital   A – B

If a business has kept very little information of its transactions it may only be possible to calculate net profit for the year. This can be done using the accounting equation as follows:

Net Assets = Capital + Profit – Drawings

Change in Net Assets = Capital introduced in period + Profit for period – Drawings in period

The change in net assets is the difference between the opening and closing net assets.

12

Statement of cash flows

In this chapter

- Benefits and presentation.
- Cash flows from operating activities.
- Cash flows from investing and financing activities.

You must learn the format as laid down in IAS7. Questions will expect you to work out relevant cash inflows/outflows under specific headings. Incomplete record techniques will need to be applied to work out missing figures.

Benefits and presentation

Definition	A statement of cash flows shows how the entity has **generated and used cash** and cash equivalents during the period.
Benefits	• Helps users of accounts to **assess** the **ability** of the entity to **generate cash**. • Helps users of accounts to **compare the performance of different entities**, because comparisons of cash flows are not affected by differences in accounting policies between entities. • Historical cash flows are often a **useful indicator** of the timing, amount and certainty of **future cash flows**.
Cash	Consists of '**cash in hand and demand deposits**' (IAS 7, para 6).
Cash equivalents	Consists of '**short-term, highly-liquid investments that are readily convertible into known amounts of cash and which are subject to an insignificant risk of changes in value**' (IAS 7, para 6).
Presentation	**IAS 7** requires companies to report cash flows for the period classified by cash flows from **operating activities, investing activities and financing activities**. It also requires a **note** showing the **components of cash and cash equivalents** and a **reconciliation** of amounts in **statement of cash flows** with amounts in **statement of financial position**.

Cash flows from operating activities

Definition	Cash flows from operating activities are the cash flows associated with the **main revenue-earning activities** of the entity.
Examples	• cash receipts from the **sale of goods and services**
	• cash receipts from sources such as **royalties and fees**
	• cash **payments to suppliers** for goods and services
	• cash **payments to employees** and on behalf of employees (for example, taxes deducted from salaries and paid to the tax authorities)
	• cash payments of **taxation** on profits.
Problem areas	Some cash flows can be classified under more than one heading:
	• **interest payments** may be classified as either an operating cash flow or a financing cash flow
	• **interest receipts and dividend receipts** may be classified as either an operating cash flow or an investing cash flow
	• **dividend payments may be treated as either** a financing cash flow or an element in the cash flows from operating activities.

Statement of cash flows for the year ended 31 December 20X7

	$	$
Net cash flow from operating activities		
Net profit before taxation	X	
Adjustments for		
Interest payable (interest expense)	X	
Depreciation/amortisation	X	
Loss on disposal of non current assets	X	
Profit on disposal of non current assets	(X)	
Operating profit before working capital changes		X
(Increase)/decrease in inventories		(X)/X
(Increase)/decrease in trade receivables		(X)/X
Increase/(decrease) in trade payables		X/(X)
Cash generated from operations		X
Interest paid	(X)	
Income taxes paid	(X)	
		(X)
Net cash from operating activities		X

Cash flows from investing activities	$	$
Purchase of property, plant and equipment/intangible non current assets	(X)	
Proceeds of sale of non current assets	X	
Interest/dividends received	X	
Net cash used in investing activities		X/(X)
Cash flows from financing activities		
Proceeds from issue of shares	X	
Receipt of loans	X	
Dividends paid	(x)	
Repayment of loans	(X)	
Net cash used in financing activities		X/(X)
Net increase/(decrease) in cash and cash equivalents		X/(X)
Cash and cash equivalents at the beginning of the period		X/(X)
Cash and cash equivalents at the end of the period		X/(X)

IAS 7 allows cash flows generated from operations to be presented in either of two ways:

- the direct method
- the indirect method.

The direct method of presenting cash flows generated from operations

Cash flows from operating activities	$000
Cash receipts from customers	x
Cash paid to suppliers	(x)
Cash paid to and on behalf of employees	(x)
Cash generated from operations	x

Figures are **derived from the accounting records** (i.e. the ledger accounts).

IAS 7 encourages, but does not require, **the use of the direct method of presenting operating activities**. In the exam you may be asked to prepare either the direct or indirect method of presenting operating activities in a statement of cash flows.

Cash flows from investing and financing activities

	Investing activities	Financing activities
Definition	Relate to sale and purchase of **non-current assets**.	Relate to issue and redemption of **equity and loan finance**.
Cash payments	• Cash payments to **acquire property, plant and equipment**. • Cash payments to **acquire intangible assets** and other long-term assets, including cash paid for capitalised development costs. • Cash paid for a **long-term investment** in another entity.	• Cash payments to **redeem/buy back shares**. • Cash payments to **repay a loan** or redeem bonds/debt securities.
Cash receipts	• Cash receipts from the **sale of property, plant and equipment**. • Cash receipts from the **sale of intangible non-current assets**. • **Dividends/interest received**.	• Cash **proceeds from issuing shares**. • Cash **proceeds from a loan** or issue of bonds/debt securities.

13

Interpretation of financial statements

In this chapter

- Interpreting financial information.
- Profitability ratios.
- Liquidity and efficiency ratios.
- Financial position.

It is important to understand the meaning of the ratios as well as calculating them for the exam.

Interpreting financial information

Introduction

Financial statements on their own are of limited use. In this chapter we will consider how to interpret them and gain additional useful information from them.

Users of financial statements

When interpreting financial statements it is important to ascertain who are the users of accounts and what information they need:

- shareholders and potential investors – primarily concerned with receiving an adequate return on their investment, but it must at least provide security and liquidity

- suppliers and lenders – concerned with the security of their debt or loan

- management – concerned with the trend and level of profits, since this is the main measure of their success.

Commenting on ratios

Ratios are of limited use on their own, thus, the following points should serve as a useful checklist if you need to analyse the data and comment on it:

- What does the ratio literally mean?
- What does a change in the ratio mean?
- What is the norm?
- What are the limitations of the ratio?

Profitability ratios

Gross profit margin

Gross profit margin or percentage is:

$$\frac{\text{Gross profit}}{\text{Sales revenue}} \times 100\%$$

This is the margin that the company makes on its sales, and would be expected to remain reasonably constant.

Since the ratio is affected by only a small number of variables, a change may be traced to a change in:

- selling prices – normally deliberate though sometimes unavoidable, e.g. because of increased competition
- sales mix – often deliberate
- purchase cost – including carriage or discounts

- production cost – materials, labour or production overheads
- inventory – errors in counting, valuing or cutoff, inventory shortages.

Operating profit margin (net profit)

The operating profit margin or net profit margin is calculated as:

$$\frac{\text{PBIT}}{\text{Sales revenue}} \times 100\%$$

Any changes in operating profit margin should be considered further:

- Are they in line with changes in gross profit margin?
- Are they in line with changes in sales revenue?
- As many costs are fixed they need not necessarily increase/decrease with a change in revenue.

- Look for individual cost categories that have increased/decreased significantly.

ROCE

$$ROCE = \frac{Profit}{Capital\ employed} \times 100\%$$

Profit is measured as:

- operating (trading) profit, or
- the PBIT, i.e. the profit before taking account of any returns paid to the providers of long-term finance.

Capital employed is measured as:

- equity, plus interest-bearing finance, i.e. the long-term finance supporting the business.

ROCE for the current year should be compared to:

- the prior year ROCE
- a target ROCE
- the cost of borrowing
- other entities' ROCE in the same industry.

Net asset turnover

The net asset turnover is:

$$\frac{Sales\ revenue}{Capital\ employed\ (net\ assets)} = times\ pa$$

It measures management's efficiency in generating revenue from the net assets at its disposal:

- the higher, the more efficient.

Note that this can be further subdivided into:

- noncurrent asset turnover (by making noncurrent assets the denominator) and
- working capital turnover (by making net current assets the denominator).

Relationship between ratios

ROCE can be subdivided into profit margin and asset turnover.

Profit margin × Asset turnover = ROCE

$$\frac{PBIT}{Sales\ revenue} \times \frac{Sales\ revenue}{Capital\ employed} = \frac{PBIT}{Capital\ employed}$$

Profit margin is often seen as an indication of the quality of products or services supplied (top of range products usually have higher margins).

Asset turnover is often seen as a measure of how intensively the assets are worked.

A trade-off may exist between margin and asset turnover.

- Low-margin businesses (e.g. food retailers) usually have a high asset turnover.

- Capital-intensive manufacturing industries usually have relatively low asset turnover but higher margins (e.g. electrical equipment manufacturers).

Two completely different strategies can achieve the same ROCE.

- Sell goods at a high profit margin with sales volume remaining low (e.g. designer dress shop).

- Sell goods at a low profit margin with very high sales volume (e.g. discount clothes store).

Liquidity and efficiency ratios

Working capital ratios

There are two ratios used to measure overall working capital:

*   the current ratio
*   the quick or acid test ratio.

Current ratio

Current or working capital ratio:

$$\frac{\text{Current assets}}{\text{Current liabilities}} : 1$$

The current ratio measures the adequacy of current assets to meet the liabilities as they fall due.

A high or increasing figure may appear safe but should be regarded with suspicion as it may be due to:

*   high levels of inventory and receivables (check working capital management ratios)
*   high cash levels which could be put to better use (e.g. by investing in non-current assets).

Quick ratio

Quick ratio (also known as the liquidity and acid test) ratio:

$$\text{Quick ratio} = \frac{\text{Current assets} - \text{Inventory}}{\text{Current liabilities}} : 1$$

The quick ratio is also known as the acid test ratio because by eliminating inventory from current assets it provides the acid test of whether the entity has sufficient liquid resources (receivables and cash) to settle its liabilities.

Inventory turnover period

Inventory turnover period is defined as:

$$\frac{\text{Inventory}}{\text{COS}} \times 365 \text{ days}$$

An alternative is to express the inventory turnover period as a number of times:

$$\frac{\text{Cost of sales}}{\text{Inventory}} = \text{times pa}$$

An increasing number of days (or a diminishing multiple) implies that inventory is turning over less quickly which is regarded as a bad sign as it may indicate:

* lack of demand for the goods
* poor inventory control
* an increase in costs (storage, obsolescence, insurance, damage).

However, it may not necessarily be bad where management are:

* buying inventory in larger quantities to take advantage of trade discounts, or
* increasing inventory levels to avoid stock-outs.

Receivables collection period

This is normally expressed as a number of days:

$$\frac{\text{Trade receivables}}{\text{Credit sales}} \times 365$$

The collection period should be compared with:

* the stated credit policy
* previous period figures.

Increasing accounts receivables collection period is usually a bad sign suggesting lack of proper credit control which may lead to irrecoverable debts.

It may, however, be due to:

- a deliberate policy to attract more trade, or
- a major new customer being allowed different terms.

Falling receivables days is usually a good sign, though it could indicate that the entity is suffering a cash shortage.

Payables payment period

This is usually expressed as:

$$\frac{\text{Trade payables}}{\text{Credit purchases}} \times 365$$

This represents the credit period taken by the entity from its suppliers.

The ratio is always compared to previous years:

- A long credit period may be good as it represents a source of free finance.
- A long credit period may indicate that the entity is unable to pay more quickly because of liquidity problems.

If the credit period is long:

- the entity may develop a poor reputation as a slow payer and may not be able to find new suppliers
- existing suppliers may decide to discontinue supplies
- the entity may be losing out on worthwhile cash discounts.

In most sets of financial statements (in practice and in examinations) the figure for purchases will not be available therefore cost of sales is normally used as an approximation in the calculation of the accounts payable payment period.

Financial position

The main points to consider when assessing the longer-term financial position are:

- gearing
- overtrading.

Gearing

Gearing ratios indicate:

- the degree of risk attached to the entity and
- the sensitivity of earnings and dividends to changes in profitability and activity level.

Preference share capital is usually counted as part of debt rather than equity since it carries the right to a fixed rate of dividend which is payable before the ordinary shareholders have any right to a dividend.

High and low gearing

In highly geared entities:

- a large proportion of fixed-return capital is used
- there is a greater risk of insolvency
- returns to shareholders will grow proportionately more if profits are growing.

Low-geared entities:

- provide scope to increase borrowings when potentially profitable projects are available
- can usually borrow more easily.

Measuring gearing

There are two methods commonly used to express gearing as follows.

Debt/equity ratio:

$$\frac{\text{Loans + Preference share capital}}{\text{Ordinary share capital + Equity reserves + Non-controlling interest}}$$

Percentage of capital employed represented by borrowings:

$$\frac{\text{Loans + Preference share capital}}{\text{Ordinary share capital + Equity reserves + Non-controlling interest + Loans + Preference share capital}}$$

Interest cover

$$\text{Interest cover} = \frac{\text{PBIT}}{\text{Interest payable}}$$

Interest cover indicates the ability of an entity to pay interest out of profits generated:

- low interest cover indicates to shareholders that their dividends are at risk (because most profits are eaten up by interest payments) and
- the entity may have difficulty financing its debts if its profits fall
- interest cover of less than two is usually considered unsatisfactory.

14

Consolidated financial statements

In this chapter

- IAS 27 Separate Financial Statements.
- Principles of accounting for investments in other entities.
- Principles of preparing consolidated financial statements.
- Group definitions.
- Fair values.
- Intra-group trading.
- Unrealised profit.
- Midyear acquisitions.

You need to understand the key terminology for group accounts and the five key workings as each of these can be tested individually.

IAS 27 Separate Financial Statements

When preparing separate financial statements, IAS 27 permits a parent entity to account for an interest in a subsidiary at cost, or at fair value or using equity accounting.

For Financial Accounting, an interest in a subsidiary is normally accounted for at cost in the separate financial statements of the parent.

Principles of accounting for investments in other entities

Subsidiary	Associate
A subsidiary is 'an entity which is controlled by another entity' (IFRS 10, App A)	An associate is 'an entity over which the investor has significant influence' (IAS 28, para 3)
Own majority of voting shares in the other entity – in excess of 50%.	Own between 20% – 50% of the shares of the other entity.
Accounting requirements: • Prepare consolidated accounts for group entities under common control. • Calculate goodwill at acquisition. • Recognise NCI if own less than 100% of shares in the other entity. • Calculate and eliminate intra-group transactions and balances between parent and subsidiary. • Calculate and eliminate any provision for unrealised profit included within inventory at the end of the year.	Accounting requirements: • Use equity accounting to account for associate in consolidated accounts. • Account for only the group share of interest in associate in P&L and SOFP.

IFRS 10 states three requirements for one entity to have control over another as follows:

(1) Power over the investee, which is normally exercised through the majority of voting rights (i.e. owning more than 50% of the equity shares).

(2) Exposure or rights to variable returns from involvement (e.g. a dividend).

(3) The ability to use power over the investee to affect the amount of investor returns. This is regarded as a crucial determinant in deciding whether or not one entity has control of another.

This is normally reflected by the parent entity holding a majority of the equity (voting) shares in another entity. When one entity has control of another, it will prepare consolidated accounts for the combined group.

Principles of preparing consolidated financial statements

The basic method of preparing a consolidated statement of financial position

(1) The assets and liabilities of the parent and the subsidiary are added together on a line-by-line basis.

(2) The investment in the parent's SoFP is replaced by a goodwill figure.

(3) The share capital and share premium balances are not added together; only the balances related to the parent are used in the consolidation.

(4) An amount attributable to non-controlling interests (NCI) is calculated and shown separately on the face of the consolidated SoFP.

(5) The group share of the subsidiary's profit is calculated and added to overall group retained earnings.

The mechanics of consolidation

A standard group accounting question will provide the accounts of P and the accounts of S and will require the calculation of various elements of the consolidated accounts.

The best approach is to use a set of standard workings.

(W1) Establish the group structure

P

Date of acquisition | 80%

S

This indicates that P owns 80% of the ordinary shares of S and when they were acquired.

(W2) Net assets of subsidiary

	At date of acquisition $	At the reporting date $
Share capital	X	X
Share premium	X	X
Retained earnings	X	X
	X	X

(W3) Goodwill

	$
Fair value (FV) of consideration paid	X
FV of NCI at acquisition	X
	—
	X
Less:	
Fair value of net assets at acquisition (W2)	(X)
	—
Goodwill on acquisition	X

(W4) Non controlling interest

	$
FV of NCI at acquisition (as in W3)	X
NCI share of post-acquisition reserves (W2)	X
	—
	X
	—

(W5) Group retained earnings

	$
P's retained earnings (100%)	X
P's % of sub's post acquisition retained earnings	X
	—
	X

The basic method of preparing a consolidated statement of profit or loss

(1) The revenue and expenses of the parent and the subsidiary are added together on a line-by-line basis.

(2) Remove the full value of intra-group trading between the parent and subsidiary during the year from both revenue and cost of sales.

(3) Calculate and remove the value of any unrealised profit in inventory at the end of the accounting period. In effect, the adjustment will lower the value of closing inventory, meaning that cost of sales will be increased.

(4) Remember that if you are dealing with the first accounting period, you may need to pro-rata the income and expenses of the subsidiary to ensure that you account only for post-acquisition trading.

Group definitions

The definition of goodwill is:

Goodwill is '**an asset representing the future economic benefits arising from other assets acquired in a business combination that are not individually identified and separately recognised**' (IFRS 3, App A)

Goodwill is calculated as the excess of the consideration transferred and amount of any non-controlling interest over the net of the acquisition date identifiable assets acquired and liabilities assumed.

Pre- and post acquisition reserves

Pre- acquisition profits are the reserves which exist in a subsidiary entity at the date when it is acquired.

They are capitalised at the date of acquisition by including them in the goodwill calculation.

Post acquisition profits are profits made and included in the retained earnings of the subsidiary entity following acquisition.

They are included in group retained earnings.

Group reserves

When looking at the reserves of S at the year end, e.g revaluation surplus, a distinction must be made between:

- those reserves of S which existed at the date of acquisition by P (pre- acquisition reserves) and
- the increase in the reserves of S which arose after acquisition by P (post acquisition reserves).

As with retained earnings, only the group share of post acquisition reserves of S is included in the group statement of financial position.

Non-controlling interest

What is a non-controlling interest?

In some situations a parent may not own all of the shares in the subsidiary, e.g. if P owns only 80% of the ordinary shares of S, there is a non-controlling interest of 20%.

Note, however, that P still controls S.

Accounting treatment of a non-controlling interest

As P controls S:

- in the consolidated statement of financial position, include all of the net assets of S (to show control).
- 'give back' the net assets of S which belong to the non-controlling interest within the equity section of the consolidated statement of financial position (calculated in W4).

Fair values

Fair value of consideration and net assets

To ensure that an accurate figure is calculated for goodwill:

- the consideration paid for a subsidiary must be accounted for at fair value

- the subsidiary's identifiable assets and liabilities acquired must be accounted for at their fair values.

IFRS 13 para 9 defines fair value as:

"The price that would be received to sell an asset or paid to transfer a liability in an orderly transaction between market participants at the measurement date."

Fair value of net assets acquired

The need to account on a fair value basis reflects the fact that the statement of financial position often values items (mainly non-current assets) at their historic cost less depreciation. This could mean the carrying value of assets is different to their current market values, particularly in the case of assets that tend to appreciate in value, such as land and buildings.

How to include fair values in consolidation workings

(1) Adjust both columns of **W2** to bring the net assets to fair value at acquisition and reporting date.

This will ensure that the fair value of net assets is carried through to the goodwill and non-controlling interest calculations.

	At date of acquisition $000	At the reporting date $000
Ordinary share capital + reserves	X	X
Fair value adjustments	X	X
	X	X

(2) At the reporting date make the adjustment on the face of the SFP when adding across assets and liabilities.

Intra-group trading

Types of intra-group trading

P and S may well trade with each other leading to the following potential problem areas:

- current accounts between P and S
- loans held by one entity in the other
- dividends and loan interest
- unrealised profits on sales of inventory.

Current accounts

If P and S trade with each other then this will probably be done on credit leading to:

- a receivables (current) account in one entity's SFP
- a payables (current) account in the other entity's SFP.

These are amounts owing within the group rather than outside the group and therefore they must not appear in the consolidated statement of financial position.

They are therefore cancelled (contra'd) against each other on consolidation.

Cash/goods in transit

At the year end, current accounts may not agree, owing to the existence of in-transit items such as goods or cash.

The usual rules are as follows:

- If the goods or cash are in transit between P and S, make the adjusting entry to the statement of financial position of the recipient:

  - cash in transit adjusting entry is:

  - Dr Cash in transit

  - Cr Receivables current account

  - goods in transit adjusting entry is:

- Dr Inventory

- Cr Payables current account

this adjustment is for the purpose of consolidation only.

- Once in agreement, the current accounts may be contra'd and cancelled as part of the process of cross casting the assets and liabilities.

- This means that reconciled current account balance amounts are removed from both receivables and payables in the consolidated statement of financial position.

Unrealised profit

Profits made by members of a group on transactions with other group members are:

- recognised in the accounts of the individual entities concerned, but
- in terms of the group as a whole, such profits are unrealised and must be eliminated from the consolidated accounts.

Unrealised profit may arise within a group scenario on:

- inventory where entities trade with each other.

Intra-group trading and unrealised profit in inventory

When one group entity sells goods to another a number of adjustments may be needed.

- Current accounts must be cancelled.
- Where goods are still held by a group entity, any unrealised profit must be cancelled.

Inventory must be included at original cost to the group (i.e. cost to the entity which then sold it).

Adjustments for unrealised profit in inventory

The process to adjust is:

(1) Determine the value of closing inventory included in an individual entity's accounts which has been purchased from another entity in the group.

(2) Use markup or margin to calculate how much of that value represents profit earned by the selling entity.

(3) Make the adjustments. These will depend on who the seller is.

If the seller is the parent entity, the profit element is included in the holding entity's accounts and relates entirely to the group.

Adjustment required:

Dr Group retained earnings (deduct the profit in **W5**) Cr Group inventory

If the seller is the subsidiary, the profit element is included in the subsidiary entity's accounts and relates partly to the group, partly to non controlling interests (if any).

Adjustment required:

Dr Subsidiary retained earnings (deduct the profit in W2 at reporting date)

Cr Group inventory

Midyear acquisitions

Calculation of reserves at date of acquisition

If a parent entity acquires a subsidiary midyear, the net assets at the date of acquisition must be calculated based on the net assets at the start of the subsidiary's financial year plus the profits of up to the date of acquisition.

To calculate this it is normally assumed that S's profit after tax accrues evenly over time.

References

The Board (2018) *Conceptual Framework For Financial Reporting*. London: IFRS Foundation.

The Board (2022) *IAS 1 Presentation of Financial Statements*. London: IFRS Foundation.

The Board (2022) *IAS 2 Inventories*. London: IFRS Foundation

The Board (2022) *IAS 7 Statement of Cash Flows*. London: IFRS Foundation

The Board (2022) *IAS 10 Events after the Reporting Period* London: IFRS Foundation.

The Board (2022) *IAS 16 Property, Plant and Equipment*. London: IFRS Foundation.

The Board (2022) *IAS 27 Separate Financial Statements*. London: IFRS Foundation.

The Board (2022) *IAS 28 Investments in Associates and Joint Ventures*. London: IFRS Foundation.

The Board (2022) *IAS 37 Provisions, Contingent Liabilities and Contingent Assets*. London: IFRS Foundation.

The Board (2022) *IAS 38 Intangible Assets*. London: IFRS Foundation.

The Board (2022) *IFRS 3 Business Combinations*. London: IFRS Foundation.

The Board (2022) *IFRS 10 Consolidated Financial Statements*. London: IFRS Foundation.

The Board (2022) *IFRS 15 Revenue from Contracts with Customers*. London: IFRS Foundation.

Index